David Ross

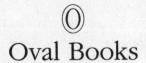

Oval Books

Published by Oval Books
335 Kennington Road
London SE11 4QE

Telephone: (0) 20 7582 7123
Fax: (0) 20 7582 1022
E-mail: info@ovalbooks.com

Editor – Catriona Tulloch Scott
Series Editor – Anne Tauté

Cover designer – Jim Wire, Quantum
Printer – Cox & Wyman Ltd

ISBN: 1-902825-42-X

Contents

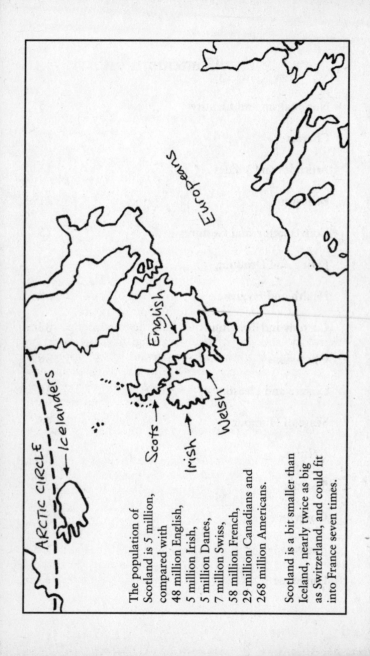

ARCTIC CIRCLE

← Icelanders

Europeans

English

Scots →

Irish →

Welsh →

The population of
Scotland is 5 million,
compared with
48 million English,
5 million Irish,
5 million Danes,
7 million Swiss,
58 million French,
29 million Canadians and
268 million Americans.

Scotland is a bit smaller than
Iceland, nearly twice as big
as Switzerland, and could fit
into France seven times.

Nationalism and Identity

Forewarned

If there is one characteristic that the Scots cherish above all others, it is that they are different. Not better than anyone else, certainly not worse, but definitely not to be confused with any other nation. A great deal of effort is put into being distinctive. Some people think this is all to do with the tourism industry, but they are quite wrong. The Scots do it entirely for their own satisfaction.

Living as they do on the north-western edge of Europe, they have evolved their own way of doing things, and take great pride in it. Even the contrasts and contradictions, of which there are many, simply become part of the story. Being Scottish is not a simple and straightforward affair: if it were, the differences would disappear. For many Scots, perfecting their Scottishness is a lifetime's activity.

This may lead you to think that the Scots are a nation addicted to showing off and boasting. Nothing could be further from the truth – they just want you to appreciate the fact that they are people who dance to their own particular tune. Like accomplished performers on the stage, they prefer a quiet, informed understanding on the part of the visitor. Knowing this enables you to appreciate their finer points: this is the essence of judgement, and all Scots are judges at heart.

It is a private fear shared among the Scots themselves that as a nation their behaviour is the product of a deep sense of inferiority. A country cannot give up its independent nationhood, as the Scots did in 1707, without a few qualms and a sharp sense of what is being lost. Even before that, Scotland was twice turned into a province of England (under Edward I, the 'Hammer of the Scots', and under Oliver Cromwell). Both times, independence was reclaimed. The Scots are used to picking themselves up and starting again – nowadays you can see this process at work in the country's regular ability to reach the World Cup Finals in soccer, only to be knocked out in the first round.

However, the fear of inferiority is misplaced. It comes from the fact that, like broadcasting from a small station against another that jams nearly all the wave-bands, the Scots have always had to shout to make their voices heard and their presence known. Otherwise the stifling proximity of England would have silenced them long ago.

Far from feeling inferior, the Scots have a very sustained and steady sense of their own worth, and they don't mind who knows it. They know that quite apart from such things as golf, whisky, tartan, bagpipe music and Dundee cake, they have given the world the first effective steam engine, gas for lighting, the bicycle, the pneumatic tyre, chloroform, the telephone, television, paraffin, penicillin, the ultra-sound scanner, the mackintosh, the milking machine, the water softener, Dolly the cloned sheep... and if you don't, they'll be glad to enlighten you. This is not a reticent, withdrawn, sorry-we've-bothered-you set of people.

How They See Others

Non-Scots are divided into two main groups: 1. The English; 2. The Rest. If you come from among The Rest, you have a head start.

The Scots like Americans, partly because many of the Americans who come to Scotland are of Scots ancestry, but more because they are intrigued by the American readiness to express admiration, wonder, puzzlement or ignorance; and by what they see as uncomplicated open-ness and generosity. Canadians are liked even better, because they are even more likely to be just a few generations away from being Scottish themselves.

The Scots also like Europeans, especially those from Scandinavia, whom they see as fellow-Northerners, sharing the northern virtues that combine individualism and community spirit. The memory of the 'auld alliance' has always given the French a special place – for centuries Scotland's ally against the country in between. The other Latin nations they are less sure about; the Mediterranean can seem further from Scotland than the Great Lakes or the Tasman Sea which border countries the Scots emigrated to and still feel a kinship with.

Estimates put the world population of Scots at around 30 million, of whom only 5 million live in Scotland. The rest are spread around the old British colonies, with the majority in North America. There are special nuclei, 'little Scotlands', in South Carolina, Eastern Canada and the South Island of New Zealand. But basically they went everywhere. Death notices in Scottish local newspapers still occasionally include the hopeful phrase 'Canadian papers please copy'.

But the Scots do like to remind themselves that they are a European nation. They look a little wistfully at other vibrant and fully independent countries whose populations are little greater or even less than that of Scotland – like Denmark, Switzerland and of course Ireland, that other Celtic nation, so similar in many ways yet so different in certain fundamentals. From the great mixer-blender of history, the Irish have emerged with fire on the outside and steel inside, the Scots exactly the opposite.

Xenophobia is not a condition that you find much in Scotland. Not only do visitors have the essential function of enabling the Scots to show how Scottish they are, they are genuinely appreciated. There is also the ancient Celtic tradition of hospitality, to be given even to the benighted enemy. 'Feast all night and feud in the morning,' says a

Gaelic proverb, and there are many travellers' tales of warm hospitality in distant glens.

The 'Auld Enemy'

Having given the world so much, usually without asking whether it wanted it, the Scots have never thought very much about what the rest of the world has given them. Either they take it for granted, or they'd rather not think about it. For of course the main conduit of innovation from outside – political, social, cultural, industrial – has always been that large country to the South, the 'Auld Enemy', England. Always more numerous, always richer, always ready to assert their superiority, the English have been thorns in the Scottish flesh for a thousand years. The Scots have learned their pride, their nationality, their characteristics good and bad, chiefly at the hands of the English, often violently. They are not about to forgive them for it.

When God created Scotland, says a favourite Scottish story, He looked down on it with great satisfaction. Finally He called the archangel Gabriel to have a look. "Just see," He said. "This is the best yet. Fine mountains, brave men, lovely women, nice cool weather. And I've given them beautiful music and a special drink, called whisky. Try some." Gabriel took an appreciative sip. "Excellent," he said. "But haven't You perhaps been too generous? Won't they be spoiled? Should there not be some drawback?" And God said: "Just wait till you see the neighbours I'm giving them."

It can come as a surprise to visitors that when the Scots watch England play in an international sporting competition, their support is likely to be given, not to England, but to the other side. Whether it's the Cricket World Cup or an international tiddlywinks contest, the Scots feel just

8

a bit more secure and more than a touch of dark enjoyment, when the English are knocked out.

The Scots are quick to sense patronage and arrogance in an English accent, especially a 'posh' one. It brings out all the latent prickliness of the Scottish character. They tend to label the English as snobbish, class-ridden, not very clever, lazy and self-satisfied. Both nations have been eyeball to eyeball for so long that what each sees of the other is more caricature than reality. But the reality is that for 250 years the Scots and the English have not fought each other on any field more bloody than a sportsfield.

How They See Themselves

The Scots like to feel that they are actually rather flamboyant and colourful people, tartan inside as well as out. They see themselves as warm-hearted, independent-minded yet communally spirited, and humorous. A favourite word for themselves is 'kindly'. It means a variety of things, all of them nice – friendly, good-humoured, easy-going, willing to share what little one has, thinking well of others, being part of the community. Well, every nation has an ideal to aspire to, and the Scots are no exception.

How They See Each Other

Scots identify one another by locality, and the cordiality when they meet outside Scotland will be all the greater if both are from Ayrshire, or Auchtermuchty. But when at home, attitudes can harden a bit. The rivalry between Edinburgh and Glasgow is famous. After their side won the European Cup in Lisbon, two Glasgow Celtic fans were hitch-hiking home. A car drew up. "We're going to Edinburgh," said the driver. "That's nae good," they said. "We're gaun tae Glesga."

In Edinburgh they regard Glasgow as a trollop of a town, brash, noisy and vulgar. The Glaswegians retaliate with their view of the typical Edinburgher, "all fur coat and nae knickers". A character in one of Neil Munro's stories says: "All the wise men in Glasgow come from the East – that's to say they come from Edinburgh." "Yes," replies a Glaswegian, "and the wiser they are, the quicker they come."

There are other rivalries, including that between the Highlanders and the Lowlanders. Ethnologically the Scots are a mixture of Celtic and pre-Celtic peoples, Nordic settlers, Anglo-Saxons, and Flemings, and contrary to what many suppose, this ancestry is shared between the Highlanders and the Lowlanders. The differences are cultural rather than ethnic, and used to be underlined by the fact that Gaelic, once the language of the whole country, continued for centuries to be spoken in the Highlands. This does not prevent the Highlanders from regarding the Lowlanders as being regimented urbanites little more civilised than the English, while the Lowlanders consider the Highlanders to be a crowd of lazy, dreamy, feckless subsidy-junkies. It was not a Highlander who composed 'The Crofter's Prayer':

Oh, that the peats would cut themselves,
The fish jump on the shore;
And that I in my bed could always lie
And sleep for evermore.

Competition and rivalry come right down to local level, and neighbouring towns often have highly un-neighbourly things to say about each other. Even within one town, people form tribal divisions. In the Orkney capital of Kirkwall, the annual 'ba' game' is fought out on New Year's Day between two sections of the town, the 'Uppies' and the 'Doonies', and no Uppie would ever dream of siding with the opposition, any more than would a Doonie.

The severest criticisms of the Scots are always reserved for one another. Nothing can beat the vituperative energy with which small, schismatic Presbyterian sects excommunicate those who step outside their narrow code. This happened to Lord Mackay, one-time Lord Chancellor, who was expelled from membership of the Free Presbyterian Church because he ventured to attend the funeral of a Roman Catholic friend. The harshest judgements, however, fall on football referees. The 'men in black' are invariably assumed by disappointed supporters of the losing team to be in diabolic conspiracy with the other side. They frequently have to leave the ground with their coats over their heads.

'As Others See Them'

The Scotsman of popular imagination is a tartan-swathed figure of heroic strength, red-haired, red-bearded and spoiling for a fight – an image which Scots are quite happy to accept, particularly the stocky, unfit, balding ones.

The Scots are not seen as a frivolous or light-hearted people: seriousness is a natural companion of the grey skies, the porridge, the craggy architecture and all that education. However, mixed in with English mockery of Scottish earnestness and pride is a substantial amount of respect. Scottish cleverness is not entirely mythical. There is a tale of a young civil servant making his first trip from Edinburgh to meet his superiors in London. When he returned, he was asked, "How did you like the English?" "I don't know," he replied. "I never met any. I only talked to Heads of Departments."

There is a hint of glamour about the Scots. For an English child, to have a Scottish granny is a definite plus:

a link to a glamorous past, a safe touch of difference to the boring norm. The French, who have also known the Scots a long time, have a saying at least as old as Rabelais, *'fier comme un Ecossais'* – as proud as a Scot. In Poland, the word 'Scot' means a pedlar, from the many Scottish packmen who once tramped its roads. The Germans in the 1914-18 war called the kilted Scottish regiments 'the ladies from Hell'.

How They Would Like To Be Seen

The Scots would like to be seen by others as they see themselves. Being Scottish, however, they don't readily reveal how they see themselves: they have to trust in the perspicacity of the visitor to see past the serious, unsmiling exterior into the romantic soul within.

Character

The Scots are a nation of polarities: sober and wild, traditional and innovative, inhibited and emotional. The tongue-twisting term 'Caledonian antisyzygy', meaning disjunction or splitting, was coined to express the contradictions in the Scottish character by a literary critic who had read such tales as Robert Louis Stevenson's *Dr Jekyll and Mr Hyde*, in which the same individual is both the kindly doctor and his fiendish alter ego.

Few people can show greater kindness and concern for misfortune than the Scots. But they also exhibit a sort of brusqueness, a touch of aggressiveness, as if they feel the world is a hostile place and they must square up to it.

Hidden Emotions

The Scottish writer John Buchan once solemnly proclaimed: "We are the most emotional nation on earth." Non-Scots must have laughed aloud, for if any nation keeps its innermost feelings to itself, it is the Scots. They will tell you a joke without smiling; they will stand silent and apparently unmoved at funerals; they will say goodbye to their dearest friends without a hint of emotion; they will communicate their love with a pat on the shoulder or a peck on the cheek. The Scots are a pretty serious lot, as if to be Scottish was a heavy responsibility. Perhaps Buchan was right after all. Dangerously tempestuous surges must lie deep beneath their stern Scottish countenances, if they are so reluctant to let them loose.

The highest form of praise ever uttered by many of them is "Not bad". A woman dressed up for an evening out might win the remark, "You're no' looking bad the night". This reticence, this curious fear of displaying ordinary human vulnerability, can sometimes lead to an unattractive gruffness. Some Scots may seem surly and unfriendly without meaning to, or at least without being able to help it. They have developed a challenging, brusque manner to protect the fragile, love-seeking spirit within, and have done it so successfully that their true self is never detected by others. Such people are often surprised at this failure to perceive their soft centre, and go through life feeling misunderstood and under-appreciated, becoming even gruffer as a result.

Two things can reliably release Scottish inhibitions. One is being abroad. The Scot abroad is infinitely more human than at home. Surrounded by people who don't mind showing their feelings, and warmed by an unfamiliar sun, the protective shell drops off. Taciturnity is replaced by garrulity, diffidence by confidence, shyness by expansive gestures, and the picture of the flamboyant Scot gains a little more colour.

The other is drinking. It may take a little more alcohol to release Scottish inhibitions than those of other peoples, but it works in the end.

Pawky and Dour

Two adjectives from their own form of the English language haunt the Scots. One is 'pawky', the other is 'dour'. Naturally, they mean opposite things. Pawky is defined in the dictionary as 'tricky, artful; dryly humorous'. The pawky Scot is a person with a droll grin and a wisecrack to accompany it. The dour Scot is a person with a grim expression, a grim mind, and a grim turn of phrase to accompany it. It is a special Scottish talent to combine both characteristics within the same person.

It was in display of his dour aspect that a husband said to his dying wife that, all right, he would have her sister to ride beside him at her funeral. "But," he added, "it'll fair spoil the day for me." The anecdote itself is a pawky one.

Canny

There is another often-perceived quality that makes the Scots wince just a little, if they are accused of having it, and that is being canny. It is one of those Scottish characteristics that tends to be misunderstood or exaggerated by non-Scots, and even the Scots themselves agree that it can be overdone.

The canny Scot is one who thinks before he speaks, and some Scottish silences are merely the pause before the plunge. Deep and different things lie behind this. The wish not to offend is an ancient trait of the Celts.

Another of equal vintage is the desire to avoid being caught making some foolish remark. The Scots are sharp judges and have long memories. One feeble utterance can mark a person down as a brainless 'numpty' for life. It's a testing environment in which you have to be clever or careful to survive unscathed.

The too-canny Scot has developed an exaggerated care about what he says or does. For him it is a danger to be in any way 'kenspeckle', or different from the crowd. 'Be cautious aye before folk' is the maxim of this individual. He may harbour opinions of the most extreme kind, but he would only utter them among those whom he knows share the same views.

There is also the canny Scot who is a prudent, careful person, mindful of how much – or how little – is in his purse and how long it has to last. Long ago, the Scots learned to husband their resources, whether financial or otherwise, in order to survive bad times, worse times, and times of real trouble, as when the English invaded. Good times made them nervous – sooner or later there would be a day of reckoning, so even more bawbees were stowed away in dark corners. Hard times were normal, and therefore easier to cope with.

However this form of canniness can be taken too far – to the kind of unScottish meanness when the unexpected guest is greeted with, "You'll have had your supper?"

Being Thrawn

There is a national impulse, not far beneath the surface, of contradiction: of uttering the opposite to what has just been said, or doing something quite unexpected, just for the sake of it. And once the Scots get an idea into their heads, it can be very difficult to remove it. These forms of bloody-mindedness merge in another national characteristic of being 'thrawn'. This almost untranslatable word combines obstinacy, assertiveness, and more than a hint of wilful perversity. It is one of the steely elements in the Scottish character, but no-one could say it has charm.

A Practical Streak

A Scots housewife is, virtually by definition, tidy, able to sew cushions or bake a cake, and make her own breakfast marmalade. She saves up ends of soap, darns her children's socks, and knows six different ways of using up yesterday's cold potatoes. A Scotsman likes to feel that, almost by instinct, he could guddle a trout (palm it out of the water) or gralloch a deer (disembowel it with his knife), even if he spends his day driving a bus or designing software.

The Scots have a definite practical streak. At one extreme this means employing old bed-ends as field gates. At the other end it means building the biggest structures ever floated on the sea.

Getting On

Every Scottish child knows the question – addressed over its head to its parents – "How is she (or he) getting on?" This means, is he or she being successful, whether this is at school or college or in a career. To fail to get on is a cardinal sin. The person asking the question invariably has a story ready about their own Jean or Sandy, who is of course getting on just fine, top of the class or joining the board of an international company. The Scots set high store by success and show a strong competitive streak.

Sometimes it's a bluff, as with the small boy who assured his parents regularly that he was top of his class.

One day they asked how many were in the class, and his answer was: "Oh, just me and another wee laddie."

Melancholia

Despite the flamboyance, the practicality and the cleverness, recollection of their Celtic heritage reminds the Scots that they have a soulful, spiritual side. They are prone to a sort of pleasantly wistful melancholia, especially when the skies are grey, or the days are at their shortest, or Scotland has just lost an international football game.

*   *   *

Attitudes and Values

Class Distinctions

The Scots like to believe that they are a relatively classless society. It is one of their best-loved myths. An eminent Writer to the Signet (a superior kind of solicitor), who has been to one of the country's great endowed schools and is a member of several exclusive clubs, such as the Honourable Company of Edinburgh Golfers at Muirfield with its years-long waiting list, is unlikely to feel he is in the same social class as an unemployed construction worker who may bear the same surname.

Class is more an economic matter than a social one. Scotland is undoubtedly an open society, otherwise 'getting on' would be much less possible. A dearly beloved Scottish tale is of a visitor to the Highlands who meets an old man digging the fields of his croft all by himself and asks what his children are doing. "Ach, well, one of them is a judge in what they call the High Court, and one of them is a professor of medicine at Oxford University. But the youngest has done very well – he's the minister of the next parish."

The Scottish aristocracy still exist and many of them still live comfortably in their castles and country houses, but they no longer dominate the scene either socially or politically. A small number own a high proportion of the Scottish landscape – something the ordinary Scot resents – but they have adjusted to a society in which football players and pop singers enjoy more prestige than they do.

Scots have an eagle eye for pretensions of any kind. 'Putting on airs' is an unforgivable sin. The classic Scottish put-down is not based on social status; it comes from perceiving an opportunity to puncture a balloon. This is irresistible to the Scottish mind. "Who is born to be hanged will never be drowned," says an old Gaelic proverb. The pay-off line is always delivered with relish. Robert Burns happened to be present when a sailor rescued a well-to-do merchant who had fallen into Greenock harbour. When the man offered his rescuer a shilling, the onlookers protested at such meanness. Burns intervened: "The gentleman best knows himself the value of his own life," he said.

The Calvinist Legacy

For a few decades in the 17th century, the Scots were possibly the most religious race on earth – fanatically so, ready to kill anyone who opposed their extreme Protestant, or Calvinist, views. Ever since, they have been winding down towards a more easy-going approach. It has taken a long time: far into the 20th century the Scottish Sunday, or Sabbath, was notorious for its extreme quiet – or dullness. A humorous versifier summed it up:

'... at least, to begin the week well,
Let us all be unhappy on Sunday.'

It was only after the arrival of television that the Scottish Sunday cracked. Nowadays, anything goes on Sunday, including football matches. After long resistance, even the Isle of Lewis, stronghold of the 'Wee Frees' (the Free Presbyterian Church), now allows the passage of a ferry boat on all seven days of the week.

The Scots are still learning how to wear the formidable cloak of Calvinism, with its terrifying or inspiring insistence on the individual's direct responsibility to God, more lightly than they have in the past. You can still encounter extremes of austere piety and wild behaviour, sometimes in the same individual. Where God seems very close, the Devil is never far away, and the Scots often seem to have a close relationship with both. They tell a story about the Day of Judgement, with the damned all gathered in Hell, while God looks down on them.

"Lord, Lord, we didna ken," they cry beseechingly.
"Weel," says God, "Ye ken noo."

The majority of active churchgoers attend the established Church of Scotland – known as the Kirk. Although Calvinist in its creed, many of the Kirk's modern ideas, including women ministers and a relaxed view of 'gay' lifestyles, would make any Presbyterian worthy of past times reach for his cursing book.

The next largest denomination is the Roman Catholic church which was never quite wiped out by the Kirk in its glory days and which was greatly enlarged by floods of Irish immigrants to the central part of the country, fleeing Ireland's famines. (Exchanges of population with Ireland are partly responsible for the religious hostility that plagues Northern Ireland and is to be seen in certain elements of life in Scotland.)

Scottish Calvinism is for most a frame of mind rather than a religious dogma, but it does not get a good press, being associated with intolerance, joylessness, fatalism and a sort of sanctimonious 'I'm better than you' attitude. Its essential teachings were once summed up as:

'You can and you can't,
You will and you won't;
You'll be damned if you do
And damned if you don't.'

Though their numbers are very small, extreme Presbyterian sects remain, particularly in remote country and island districts. Their pronouncements attract news coverage, not because their views are widely shared, but just because they are now so different to the easy-going norm. Yet Calvinism is still deeply ingrained in the Scottish soul. A Scottish poet told of how, overcome by the joy of sunshine and blue sky, he cried out what a fine day it was. The woman to whom he spoke replied, "We'll pay for it, we'll pay for it."

Thrift

Ostentatious display of wealth is frowned on in Scotland, though people can get away with it if they are also 'characters'. Even when they have money, the Scots don't flaunt it. They save it.

Thriftiness is a national habit. It was after all a Scottish minister who started the world's first Savings Bank for his parishioners. The Scots were always poor, always had to count their pennies carefully. Their wealthier neighbours could not help noticing, and making humorous comments. To the Scots themselves, there was nothing very funny about this. Money was and is a serious matter. It is not a coincidence that a Scotsman should have started the Bank of England; or that Edinburgh should today be Europe's third most important financial centre (after Frankfurt and London). The Scots like bargains, but not bargaining; they are suspicious of something for nothing.

Thrift should not be confused with meanness, of which the Scots do not approve. A Scotsman sitting down to breakfast at a guesthouse and eyeing the modest dod of honey given him for his toast, looked at the proprietor and said: "I see you keep a bee."

Pride

The Scots' sense of pride, so easily ruffled by external criticism, can turn into a form of arrogance known as the 'Wha's like us?' tendency. Often it has a theatrical quality, or a hint of self-mockery, which prevents it from being taken too seriously. The most notable exponent of this was a chief of the Clan MacNeil from the island of Barra in the Outer Hebrides. Each day, when he had finished his dinner, he sent his trumpeter up to the topmost tower of his castle, where he blew a flourish and announced to the empty grey seas: "The MacNeil of Barra has dined! The rest of the world may dine."

Behaviour

A Nation of Non-conformists

The Scots are not a particularly conformist lot. This goes along with those quiet, firmly held opinions. With their strong sense of community, both local and national, they are generally law-abiding, as long as the laws make sense to them. Any hint of exploitation raises their hackles, and they have a great dislike of officious people who take it on themselves to tell others what to do. Such folk are liable to be put down with remarks like, "Does your mother ken ye're oot?"

They are quite good at queuing, if only to make sure that nobody steals a march on them, but are not the sort of people to wait for a green light to appear at the road crossing if there is no traffic coming. Instead, they often play a form of 'chicken' to see who can be last across before the traffic comes sweeping through.

Those responsible for attracting foreign companies to invest in Scotland make much of the 'Protestant work ethic' which is supposed to guarantee a dedicated and docile work force. In fact the Scots, though not averse to hard work, are far from docile as a work force. They are deeply suspicious of such concepts as 'human resource management', and relations between employers and employees are often strained.

In most activities they are unhurried. People will stop and gossip in the street. Shop assistants will chat to customers, even when people are waiting to be served. This is true even in the big cities, and when you reach the West Highlands, time ceases to have its familiar meaning. The *ceilidh* (shindig) advertised for 9 o'clock in the village hall may start getting under way by 11.00. On the isle of Mull, they say "There are no half-hours", and on the Isle of Eigg, asked when the steamer was due a local replied, "Weel, she'll be coming sometimes sooner, and whiles earlier, and sometimes before that again."

The Scots set store by good public behaviour, perhaps because most of them live in towns and cities, often in apartment blocks known as tenements, with shared responsibilities for keeping the public areas clean and tidy. It is a land of neat front gardens, scrubbed doorsteps and polished front doors. Round the back may be a tip of empty bottles and old fridges, but round the back is out of sight.

As a people they can be quite formal, and the easy, almost instant use of a first name, so common in England and America, is much less frequent. Taxonomists by nature, the Scots like to classify you. A whole mental catalogue of social reference points is brought out in readiness. After the initial inspection, they will ask you questions, designed to elicit, more or less discreetly, what sort of person you are. After they have filed you appropriately, they may talk about other things.

At the same time, a lady on a Glasgow bus is likely to be addressed by the driver as 'hen': "Will ye move up, hen, and make room furra rest of 'em?" And if you get a seat, your neighbour, after the routine swift inspection, is quite likely to start a conversation, if only to say "It's awfie cauld the day."

'Characters'

A common observation in Scotland is that "None of the old characters are left any more" which is often said by people who are obviously just as much 'characters' as those they say are no longer around.

'Characters' are essentially the same sort of people as all other Scots, except that they have somehow escaped the national qualities of reserve and seriousness. They behave in outrageous ways, often saying exactly what they think in forcible terms, or embracing people in public. Much admired, they are not envied. There are more characters around, in all walks of life, than you would suppose on first meeting the Scots. In fact, you come to realise that if the Scots were to shed their seriousness, they would be noisier than the Neapolitans and wilder than the Dervishes. Their reserve is not a defence against

23

the rest of the world: it is a protective cover, like the lid of a nuclear reactor.

The Family

The majority of Scottish mothers have a job, even if it's only part-time. Running a family has become a part-time activity. As a result, the cohesion of the once mother-centred family life has suffered. Mothers, however, remain the chief influence on their children, in charge of all day-by-day activity and of the household budget. Father traditionally brought home his pay-packet, was given some of it back, and repaired to the pub or the football stadium. He would no more have thought of helping with the cooking or housework than of walking on the ceiling. This attitude survives, and many men still regard 'women's work' as beneath their dignity. In a close-to-home tale, a Scottish couple win a million pounds in the National Lottery. "At last," says the wife, "I won't have to sweep the stairs with that old broom any more." "Of course not, hen," replies her husband. "Now I can afford to get you a new one."

The Scottish reluctance to display emotion means that relationships between parents and children can seem more off-hand than they really are. Families are quite close-knit and family feeling is strong. In the cities, many young adults continue to live in the parental home while working or studying, instead of opting for an independent lifestyle in a flat.

Care of the elderly is at a high level. They are far from being a forgotten or isolated part of society. An important factor in family life is Granny. Granny often lives quite near to her grown-up children, perhaps only one or two streets away, and plays a big part in the lives of her grandchildren, giving them their 'tea' (early evening meal) and taking them to the park. This role is good both for the children and for Granny herself, who features prominently in many children's playground songs, like 'Ye canna shove yir Granny aff a bus'.

Conversation and Gestures

There are two gestures often seen in Scots conversation. One is to separate the two hands as widely as possible. This is to demonstrate the size of the fish that the speaker almost caught. The other is to bring forefinger and thumb so close together they almost touch. This is to illustrate how close the speaker's golf ball got to the hole without going in.

Apart from the essential exchanges about the weather, it can be hard work conversing with a Scot. But, as with many people who are quite slow to start a conversation, it can be difficult to get a Scot in full flow to stop. They are often alarmingly well-informed, and the more remote the community, the truer this is likely to be.

The secret of conversation is to display ignorance, or to get an argument going. The former is safer, the second is altogether more lively. As soon as you have expressed a firm opinion on any subject from global warming to driving standards, your Scottish friend will seize on it like a terrier, shake it around, and convince you that you are utterly mistaken.

Once the conversation is well under way, and a good argument is being had, the jabbing forefinger comes into play. The Scots like to make a point as forcibly as possible, and can quickly become exasperated if it does not seem to be getting home. It can be safest in the end just to agree.

As an idea develops, it can lead the logical Scottish

mind down strange paths. Scepticism is often taken about as far as it can go. It was David Hume, the country's most celebrated philosopher, who showed the Scottish gift for taking a point of view to a stage where it is unprovable either way, of no practical use, but mentally highly satisfying. There is an abstract and intellectual quality to the Scots mind that rejoices in uncomfortable thoughts. A true Scot would sooner be right than rich, any time.

Greetings and Toasts

For the stranger, the most baffling of the greetings the Scots exchange with one another is this:

First Scot: "Aye aye."
Second Scot: "Aye."

It may be rich in meaning, depending on the use of inflection, position of the eyebrows, and movement, if any, of the lips. It can communicate anything from 'Not you again', to 'How nice to see you'. It is possible that it is also the origin of the American 'Hi'.

The Scots have ritual exchanges. When offering the national drink, a Scot will not say, "Would you like a whisky?" but "Will you take a dram?" To which the most proper answer is "Oh, just a sensation". This means, yes please, a big one. If you don't want a big one, the answer is "Oh, just a wee sensation".

Matters are not over once the glass is in your hand. Your host raises his and utters the words: "*Slainte mhath*". This is Gaelic for 'Good health' (pronounced more or less 'slanjah-vah') and is about as much Gaelic as the majority of Scots know. The correct response is "*Slainte mhór*" (pronounced 'slanjah-vore'), which means 'Great health'. Salutations may end at this point and quaffing begin, or the host may cap you with "*Slainte gu síorraidh*" ('slanjah-ga-shorrah'), which means 'Health for ever'.

The custom of the *deoch an doruis*, or drink at the door, before leaving is not common nowadays, because of tough enforcement of drink-driving laws. And the 'full Highland honours', where everyone stands with one foot on their chair and the other on the table, drains a full glass, then tosses it into the fireplace, is reserved for extremely special occasions.

Eating and Drinking

The Food

Scotland is not one of the great culinary centres of the world. Until quite recently, Scottish catering was something to be feared; visitors came despite the food. An 18th-century visitor to an Edinburgh chop-house observed that the cook was so filthy, that if you threw him against the wall, he would have stuck to it.

Nowadays, the cooks are kept out of sight, and standards have dramatically improved. The Scots have learned to exploit their own distinctive traditions in this area as in all others. An array of local specialities beckons from the menus – porridge and kippers at breakfast, soups like Cullen Skink and Cock-a-leekie, curious vegetable combinations like clapshot and stovies. But there is no cause for alarm. Essentially, Scotland excels in good plain fare – fresh fish, oatcakes, smoked salmon, roast beef, potatoes. The Scots firmly believe they grow the world's best potatoes. There is said to be a hotel in the north-east which has a potato-list as well as a wine-list; you select your preference from among the many varieties: Kerr's Pink, Catriona, Shaft's Express, Sutton's

Abundance, Maris Piper, Duke of York (both White and Red) – the waiter will advise if necessary.

The haggis was probably imported to Scotland a thousand years ago by the Vikings. It suits a frugal nation whose sheep population is about the same as the human population. Traditionally encased in a sheep's stomach, and boiled in a pot, haggis is a pudding of minced-up mutton remnants and offal, with oatmeal, onions and spices. One food writer perceptively remarked that the use of the paunch of the animal gave 'the touch of romantic barbarism so dear to the Scottish heart'. In fact, it is a very tasty dish, and many countries have something similar – it took the Scots to turn it into a tradition.

The Scots do eat their traditional dishes, but almost always at home. When they go out to eat, they become international, and head for a Chinese or Indian or Mexican or Turkish restaurant. They are also a great people for take-aways, known as 'cairry-oots'. The fish and chip shop is highly popular, and its range usually extends to oriental food as well as such uniquely Scottish delicacies as haggis in batter and the deep-fried Mars Bar.

Perhaps the cold, damp winters have something to do with it, but the Scots are one of the most sweet-toothed peoples on earth. They eat more sweet biscuits and cakes per head of the population than any other nation. In Scotland you will find a whole range of sweet products and bakery items that are unknown elsewhere. Baking is one aspect of their culinary tradition that the Scots are quite proud of, some ascribing it to the cultural influence of France, which may well be true – the breakfast 'buttery' is certainly a cousin of the croissant. There are floury rolls, baps, scones, oatcakes and many pastries, including the Scotch Pie, a savoury mutton pie, and the Forfar Bridie, a monster handful of pastry packed with meat, vegetables and gravy.

The family meal of 'high tea', served at any time

between 5 and 7 o'clock, consists of a cooked first course, eaten with bread and butter, followed by a formidable array of scones, buns, shortbread and cake, all washed down with copious amounts of well-sugared tea.

The Drink

As many people have noted, the Scots are partial to their 'bevvy'. Only confectionery is more widely on sale than alcohol, and pubs are open throughout the day. The Scottish pub, once a cheerless, sawdust-floored, guilt-inducing place, is often nowadays quite pleasant and may even have tables and seats. Partly because of the ready availability, public drunkenness is much rarer than used to be the case. But there are many serious drinkers.

Whisky is a great source of argument and discussion among the Scots. Two eminent scholars once fell into ferocious dispute, one claiming that the other had said two shocking things – first, that whisky was brought to Scotland from Ireland; second, that the Irish had used it as an embrocation for sick mules and it took the Scots to apply it to internal consumption.

For most people the talk centres on 'single malt' whiskies, and whether those from the heathery glens of the East are superior to those from the salt-sprayed coasts of the West, or vice versa. Both have their devotees, and a good Scottish host will make sure that he has a supply of each, plus perhaps one from Orkney and another from one of the Highland distilleries. Each brand has its own aroma and a 'tradition' lovingly elaborated by generations of public relations consultants. Inevitably, a mystique has grown, or been cultivated, around malt whisky. The Scots, who will cheerfully pour a hefty slug of lemonade into their glass of blended whisky, are apt to put on a face of solemn horror if you 'adulterate' malt in the same way. Some say that malts should be drunk neat. Others insist that the addition of a little water brings out the aroma and flavour.

The maturing stocks of Scotch whisky are said to be more valuable than the bullion in the Bank of England. Whisky is by far Scotland's biggest export, despite determined efforts by many Scots to consume the whole output.

Scottish beer is a puzzle to an incomer. There is a range of oddly named dark ales – eighty shilling (80/-), sixty shilling (60/-), and small, menacing bottles containing a brew known as a 'wee heavy'. These beers can be drunk on their own, but their true function is to a be chaser to whisky. Many pub drinkers have in front of them two glasses from which they drink alternately, a large one of beer and a small one of whisky. Called 'a-half-and-half', this is one of the most lethal mixtures known to man.

A small quirk which underlines Scotland's differentness is that it is the only country in the West where Coca-Cola is not the most popular soft drink. The Scots go instead for a local product called 'Irn Bru', whose by-line is 'made from girders'.

Health and Hygiene

Well entrenched in the Scottish persona is the belief that the Scots are a hardy lot, immune to the ailments which afflict weaker nations. But the reality is very different. "The typical Scot has bad teeth, a good chance of cancer, a liver under severe stress and a heart attack pending." The speaker was exaggerating for effect, but there is more than an element of truth in this. The Scots' love of sweet things doesn't do their teeth any good – it's a country where dentists do well.

A very high number fall victim to heart attacks. A Glasgow golf club has become the first non medical institution to install a defibrillator machine, to revive sufferers from heart failure. And, in a country which produces one of the world's most popular spirituous drinks, it is no surprise that alcoholism is a problem. Average life expectancy for the Scot at birth is still two years less than it is for the English and Welsh.

However, Scotland is a good country in which to be ill. It has a long tradition of medical education and expertise. The Scots were pioneers in anatomy, anaesthetics and gynaecology; they have many excellent free hospitals and produce many doctors (not all of whom are exported).

The national interest in the workings of the mind has prompted many Scots to become psychologists and psychiatrists. It was a Scottish 'shrink' who, applying a typically Scottish thought-process to his subject, came up with the concept that 'madness may not just be breakdown. It may also be breakthrough'. In his view, you'd be mad not to be mad.

Cleanliness

Hygiene is something of an issue in Scotland. Edinburgh is never allowed to forget its ancient custom of tossing sewage out of upper windows into the street. In the old days, hygiene used to play a secondary role to the need to keep warm. Many a Scottish child was sewn into its winter underwear in November and kept it on until March.

Today, most people have central heating and modern bathrooms, in which the bath is the centrepiece – they like a good wallow. But old habits die hard: whilst many Scots bath or shower every day, a sizeable proportion still clings to the idea that once a week is quite enough.

Custom and Tradition

In a world where people increasingly dress the same, eat one another's food, forget their own folklore and travel the globe to see reconstructed versions of other peoples' customs, the Scots hold several trump cards.

Their men and boys can dress up in a highly distinctive national costume. They maintain the bagpipe, a musical instrument largely abandoned by the rest of Europe in the 14th century (and defined by one critic as 'the missing link between music and noise'). They have traditional dances which add to the gaiety of festive occasions. They have ritual gatherings known as Highland Games, with piping and dancing competitions, and at which feats of strength such as tossing the caber are practised (not so long ago it was wrenching the legs off a newly slaughtered cow).

To all this, add golf, salmon-fishing, deer-stalking, grouse-shooting – each one an activity ingrained with its own lore and tradition. Lay on top the exploits of such historic figures as William Wallace, Robert the Bruce, and Bonnie Prince Charlie, and you have a tourist executive's dream: Theme Park Scotland.

The surprising thing is that, to a large extent, it is real. The Scots go to their offices and factories, schools and shops, wearing the same chain-store clothes as every other nation. You will rarely, if ever, see a kilt on the street. But go to a wedding or a ball, a university graduation or an international rugby match, and you will see any number of kilts, with perhaps an inch or two of the wearer's pale, hairy knees exposed between the kilt and the thick woolly socks.

At parties and dances people leap to their feet for Scottish dancing. Most Scots can manage the simpler dances, like 'Strip the Willow' and 'The Gay Gordons', the men lumbering gallantly into action, usually steered by the women who are better at it (the macho tradition of school playgrounds having made boys chary of going to Scottish dancing classes). For the more complicated 'reels', the band usually provides a caller, but the hardest ones, like the 'Reel of the 51st Highland Division' are best left to those who really know their intricacies.

Even the Highland Games which are hugely enjoyed by visitors would not survive if they were not also enjoyed and supported by their local communities. The Scots have the splendid luxury of being able to play at being Scottish, as well as actually being Scottish.

Clans

Clans are another part of the game of being Scottish that the Scots so much enjoy. The word clan originally meant 'children', meaning the descendants of a single person, and each clan claims descent from a single Adam-like ancestor. In the case of some clans, it is Adam himself. When a Macleod and a MacLean were disputing the age of their respective clans, Macleod said, "We never saw you on board Noah's ark." To which Maclean replied: "Who ever heard of a MacLean that didn't have his own boat?"

Once upon a time, the clansmen would obey the war signal of the Fiery Cross, take their 'claymores', or broadswords, from their hiding place in the thatch and follow their chief into battle. Nowadays, though there is a Standing Conference of Clan Chiefs, the chieftains have no authority of any sort. Many have formed Clan Associations, and some of the larger ones, like the MacDonalds or the Campbells, have a well-organised international network with regular newsletters, web sites and gatherings. They are harmless, indeed socially valuable organisations, far removed, in the case of such clans as the MacGregors and Robertsons, from their warlike

33

forebears who used to go cattle-raiding far afield, terrorising farmers and villagers. But these old stories of derring-do still put a swing in the modern clansman's kilt.

Tribalism

Before there were clans in Scotland and for a much longer period, there were tribes. The clans, in fact, represent a partial survival of the ancient tribal organisation. In the behaviour and character of modern Scots, the remnants of tribal attitudes still colour much of their views and lives. This can be seen in their attachment to the land itself, especially their own area of it, in their clannishness, in their fondness for tradition and small rituals, in their long historic memories, in their competitive spirit.

Much of the jigsaw of Scottish character drops into place when you bear in mind that the Scot is still, and quite unconsciously, a tribesman or woman at heart.

Kilts and Tartans

In ancient times Highlanders wore kilts (whose Gaelic name means 'little wrap') and plaids ('big wrap'), dyed using natural dyes, and woven in the Highlands. They were usually of striped or checked design known in Gaelic as tartan, but not of any single or defining pattern. In battle, clansmen threw off their plaids and fought in their shirts.

Tartan, or plaid, has been in existence for thousands of years. Some intriguing archaeological finds of woven cloth in eastern Europe and the Far East show just how far back in time the Celtic love of colour goes. Yet today's plethora of brightly coloured tartans dates from the 19th century with the surge of romantic interest in

Scotland and the Highlands that was vastly encouraged by Queen Victoria's visits to her castle of Balmoral (which she carpeted in tartan, of course). Not slow to spot an excellent marketing opportunity, the tailors of Edinburgh commissioned tartans for every clan name, and sold them to a public all too ready to believe that they were the real thing. Thousands of different tartans have been devised: according to one authority, there are 58 for 'Stewart' alone.

There are craggy Highland lairds who hold that one should never wear the kilt outside the Highlands. There are those who say you should only wear it if you can prove your connection to the clan whose tartan you are wearing. But the genial folk who run Highland-dress shops cut briskly through all this flim-flam. They have name charts to show that just about everyone is connected to a Scottish Highland clan.

The Scotsman in his kilt, whether he is at a society wedding or one of the Tartan Army that follows the nation's football team, acquires an extra touch of swagger: he has become a colourful figure, with a *skean dhu* (dagger) in his stocking and money in his sporran, and plays up to it with enthusiasm:

Queen Victoria: "Is anything worn beneath the kilt?"
Highlander: "No, ma'am, it's all in perfect working order."

It is difficult to be dour in a kilt.

Burns Night

Of the many icons with which the Scots surround themselves, one of the most powerful is the enduring cult of the country's National Bard.

Once a year, on Robert Burns's birthday, 25th January, hundreds of thousands of Scots throughout the world sit down to a Supper in his honour. A highly ritualised event, it involves a piper preceding the cook who bears a dish of haggis (Scots in the British Embassy in Washington have been known to have it flown in by diplomatic bag to avoid American food-import rules), the recital of Burns's *Address to a Haggis* and the ceremonious dirking (cutting open with a knife) of the pudding. Only then is the haggis consumed.

After the meal, there is a toast to the Immortal Memory of Burns himself. The diners follow this speech with intense interest, perhaps because of their deep familiarity with the poet's works, but more likely because each table has organised a sweep on the length of the speech. Toasts, including 'The Lassies' and the 'Reply to the Lassies', follow. Burns having been a notable drinker, many emulate him as a further tribute.

Hogmanay

The Scots have taken out a patent on New Year's Eve, called it Hogmanay, and achieved the astonishing feat of making icy Edinburgh a tourist centre in mid-winter. The old Northern festival of Yule was never forgotten in Scotland. It was an important point in the calendar, marking the middle of winter. The days were at their darkest, nights were at their longest – it was a wonderful excuse for a party.

With its old half-magic associations all but forgotten, the party has got bigger. Whisky, bagpipes, 'Auld Lang Syne', and Black Bun (a New Year cake described by Robert Louis Stevenson as 'a dense black substance, inimical to life') all make it special. In many places the revels have moved from the firelit hearths of people's homes to the bonfires and fireworks of public parks, with gatherings numbered in tens of thousands.

As a result, the old custom of 'first-footing' (first across the threshold after the midnight bells) has gone into a decline, except in the smaller towns and villages, where partying from house to house still goes on into the early hours, though not many Scotsmen nowadays set off to their neighbour's carrying a lump of coal and wisp of straw intended to ensure warmth and prosperity in the new year ahead.

'Auld Lang Syne'

English speakers throughout the world link hands at the end of an evening's celebration to sing these words, mysterious and incomprehensible to many. Translated from Scots to English, the title would be 'Days of Long Ago'; but its magic would be lost. Like all tribal chants, the sense of the words is less important than the feeling of togetherness they create.

Nessie

An ancient legend tells how, in the 6th century, St Columba met a monster in the River Ness and sent it packing. He was so successful that nothing more was heard of it until the 1930s, when there was a rash of claimed 'sightings' which have continued ever since.

Several books have been written on Nessie and many investigations made – all inconclusive. Just because a monster is not found, say the believers, does not mean it does not exist. Meanwhile, the local economy has benefited to an enormous extent from monster-spotters. Many locals genuinely believe there is 'something' in the loch. Others are equally convinced that it is all humbug. Not until the loch, 20 miles long and over 600 feet deep, is emptied will the controversy die down.

Obsessions

Themselves

One of the first things that the visitor realises is that the Scots are quite obsessively Scottish. It is not just that they are different and they want you to notice it, it's that Scottishness itself is a hot topic.

The Scots know who they are, but they don't know what they are. In the days when they ran the British Empire for the English, this didn't matter, but now that England is once again Little England, many Scots are wondering furiously what they are for.

No-one has yet come up with an answer, but the problem ensures that the Scots maintain their serious expressions.

The Weather

It's a good idea to have a comment on the weather ready, in case you talk to someone, or someone talks to you. The weather is a constant source of conversation. This is remarkable, given that Scotland only offers two main types of weather, wet or dry, with the sub-attributes of windy or not windy. The permutations offered by these are quite enough for meaningful communication. You may make the opening gambit: "A bit wet today", to which the reply may be, "Aye, but not so windy." Or you may choose to start with the wind, or lack of it: "It's a nice, fresh breeze", to which the reply may be, "Aye, a grand day." On days when it is both wet and windy, people just look at one another from under their rain-hats, and say: "Oh, my!"

Fine rain is referred to as 'Scotch mist', and a Scottish proverb says, 'A Scotch mist will wet an Englishman to the skin'. Another well-known piece of weather lore runs:

'If you can't see Ben Nevis, it means that it's raining. If you can see Ben Nevis, it means that it's about to rain.'

The News

The world's most voracious consumers of newsprint must be the Scots. At least nine morning and evening newspapers are published in Scotland, as well as four Sunday ones, all in addition to the 'national' British newspapers, many of which have a special Scottish edition. This is a point of pride – an advertising slogan for the *Sunday Times Scotland* read: 'The English just don't get it'.

Scotland has its own branch of the BBC (always under pressure for not broadcasting enough Scottish news), three independent television stations, and numerous local radio stations.

The Scots love to read about themselves, and every community has at least one local weekly newspaper where local news takes priority. The apocryphal tale of the Aberdeen newspaper which published the headline, 'Aberdeen Man Drowned in Atlantic. *Titanic* Sinks' is true, if only in spirit.

Football

One of the reasons they are so keen on the news is to keep up with everything that is happening in Scottish football. Among Europeans, the Scots watch more club football matches than any other country except Albania.

On Saturdays, still the day of most football matches, you can detect a different tone in the newsreader's voice. International items of the deepest import are hurried through with scant regard. The nation is waiting for the real news – the results of the Scottish Football League.

As a founder of the international game, the Scots have managed to be treated as a real national side despite not being an independent nation. Scotland has a full pattern of national soccer, from the Premier League down to the Third Division. Scottish football is a tribal business, with fierce local loyalties. In the case of Rangers and Celtic, two Premier League teams who confront each other in Glasgow, there is a lingering element of Protestant and Catholic rivalry. A local definition of an atheist is someone who supports neither one side nor the other. A similar rivalry occurs in Edinburgh between Heart of Midlothian and Hibernian. Even without this element, a local derby, as between Dundee and Dundee United, calls forth deep emotions. The football terracing is a zone where the Scots freely indulge their feelings.

Football is a passion for many Scots for whom it is the national game in a way that golf is not. It was a Scottish football manager who said, "Some people think football is a matter of life or death. I can tell them it's more serious than that." In the annual international with England especially, real nationalistic fervour moves the Scottish supporters, as though the battles of Bannockburn or Flodden were being refought each time.

Leisure and Pleasure

Helped by the fact that their cities are surrounded by beautiful open countryside, the Scots take their leisure seriously. And they have a wonderful range of activities to choose from. What is most remarkable, in a country where winter lasts from October to April, and summer has been referred to as a weekend in July, is that nearly all their leisure activities are outdoor ones. An American wit commented that "If the Scots knew enough to stay indoors when it rained, they would never get any exercise".

Golf and Games

Try telling a Scot that golf originated in Holland if you want to provoke a vigorous if localised disturbance. The Scots have absolutely no doubt about which side of the North Sea the game began on. This is the great national game for all ages and both sexes to actually play, rather than watch, and in Scotland, where every village has a golf course, it need not be expensive.

In the Borders, rugby is the game, and the farmers and millworkers of this region provide many of the players for the Scottish international side that has won its fair share of Grand Slams against the other rugby nations.

A less well-known international sport, though becoming more popular in the Northern world, and recently admitted to the Olympics, is curling, akin to bowls, but played by sending heavy granite stones scudding across the ice. Known as 'the roaring game', it is more often than not played in indoor arenas where the ice is more reliable. In the Highlands they have a wild stick-and-ball game called shinty which is similar to Irish hurling but a bit less restrained. Players have been known to scrape their opponents' eyebrows off their shinty sticks after a particularly close-fought tackle.

Central to all these activities is the club and the club-house. Indeed, the novelist Eric Linklater said the only thing he had against golf was that it took you so far from the clubhouse. Scottish sportsmen are a clubbish lot. They enjoy discussing their sport over a whisky in the club bar; some, arguing comfortably over the rules and who did what in some famous competition, never get beyond it. The epitome of all this is at St Andrews, where

41

the mandarins of the Royal and Ancient Club (or R&A) maintain the world headquarters of golf. There are six golf courses at St Andrews. The celebrated Old Course can be hard to get on to, but impecunious students at the town's university have been known to get up at 5 o'clock on a summer morning and get a free round in before the greenkeepers have had breakfast.

Skiing and Climbing

The Scots do their best to pretend that their mountains are skiable in winter, even if this involves bumping over squashy remnants of snow with grassy tufts poking through. After all, it's much nearer and sometimes cheaper than going to the Alps.

But what the mountains undoubtedly offer is magnificent rock climbing and hill walking. Each Scottish peak has been classified as either a 'Munro' (3,000 feet plus) or a 'Corbett' (2,500 feet plus), and although anyone who goes in for 'Munro-bagging' is the subject of some mirth, it is the lifetime ambition of many to climb them all.

Scottish climbers like to perpetuate a 'hard' man or woman image, and their mountain 'bothies' (stone-built shelters) are spartan places. Though it is now rare to find completely new routes up the crags, there is strong competition between clubs from the different cities. Some of the finest challenges are the cliffs and rock stacks of the coast, where the natural perils are increased by the fulmars which nest on the ledges and practise projectile vomiting into the faces of unsuspecting climbers.

Hunting, Shooting and Fishing

Another favourite pastime is fishing, preferably practised standing up to the waist in a river for several hours on end, or sitting in a small boat in a cloud of midges.

In Scotland you can fish freely for brown trout, but if you happen to catch a salmon without having a licence, don't be surprised if a gamekeeper leaps out from behind a tree – especially as salmon are by no means as plentiful as they once were. There is an old Highland saying which goes, 'A deer from the hill, a salmon from the river, and a stick from the forest is the birthright of every Gael', but many a poacher has languished in jail from trying to put it into practice.

Deer-stalking, grouse and pheasant-shooting are much more exclusive pursuits, requiring the right social or business connections, or lots of money. Once the preserve of a landowner and his guests, bird shoots are now very often let to syndicates. The locals view these activities with an amused eye. An impartial observer remarked of the shooters and the amount of cash they had to part with: "They were stung by everything and everyone."

Deer-stalking can involve spending the best part of a day crawling on your stomach across a mountainside, through heather and sticky black patches of bogland with a 'gillie' (or keeper) hissing angrily each time your head rises above the level of the plants, only to find the wind has changed and wafted your scent to the deer, who have moved with effortless ease to the other side of the hill.

'Gillie' literally means boy, but the gillie who accompanies you on stalking or loch-fishing is more likely to be a grizzled elder, encased in tweed jacket and those baggy tweed breeches known as plus-fours, economical with words, impervious to the weather and the insect life, and oozing the grittier national characteristics from every pore. When the lunch-box is opened, or the day is over, he will gravely accept a stiff dram from your flask, and may unbend so far as to utter those Scots words of praise for your day's performance: "No' bad".

Holidays

The era of mass jet travel has enabled the Scots to discover an astral object that they knew little about – the sun. In summer the Scottish population of the Canary Isles probably exceeds that of the Orkneys. It's not just the promise of unlimited sunshine and cheap wine that attracts them – it's the release of being abroad.

Once the wealthier Scots went abroad and the less well-off stayed in Scotland and went on trips "doon the watter" on the Clyde steamers. Nowadays the wealthier ones have holiday houses in coastal villages or time-share apartments in ex-baronial castles and spend their holidays in Scotland, while the majority happily buy package tours to the sun.

Sex

A well-known Scottish joke is that ladies in the smarter districts of Glasgow or Edinburgh think that sex is something the coal comes in – a jibe at their over-refined pronunciation of 'sacks'. Sex is obviously something the Scots indulge in, or there wouldn't be any of them. But when, and how? Scotland is still emerging from the repressive fog of Victorian attitudes, when piano legs were clothed, and sexual intercourse was unmentionable. The national attitude to sex is still a somewhat guarded one. As one observer concluded: "The Scots fornicate gravely but without conviction."

There was an old-established courting tradition called 'bundling', in which the young and not yet betrothed couple might spend the night together, in the girl's parental home, free to do everything short of actual consummation. Needless to say, there were many 'accidents'. In Scottish country areas, illegitimacy was never a great slur, even when moral attitudes were much more extreme than they are now.

Scotland has never made a heavy issue of marriage. Until the rest of the world caught up, it was easier both to get married and to get unmarried in Scotland than elsewhere. For a long time the sanction of the church or the registrar was not necessary in order to wed: all you needed were two witnesses – hence the large number of runaways who eloped from England to marry in the first village in Scotland, Gretna Green.

There has always been a ribald, raunchy streak somewhere in the Scottish character which emerges in the bawdier poems of Robert Burns, but there is little romance. Romance to the Scots means the dreamy Celtic past rather than modern relationships. To many Scots, particularly males, sex remains a furtive affair. Tenderness and open affection do not arise naturally. Seduction is rough-and-ready rather than loving, requiring considerable amounts of alcoholic encouragement in the preliminary stages.

Sense of Humour

It is easy to know when a Scot is telling you something funny. The face assumes an extra solemnity; the voice becomes drier; the tone more sepulchral. It's as if, in Scotland, they think that God doesn't have a sense of humour, and they must not be seen to make a joke. Or to laugh in response to one. A quick grimace is safest. Like other emotional signals, humour is kept under tight covers.

There is no nonsense or fantasy in Scottish humour. There is always a point, and frequently a moral. It has an earthy streak, like the tale of the country tramp who specialised in begging from farmhouses. Picking up a dried-up cow-turd, he would knock at the door and request some dry bread to make a 'piece', or sandwich, of it. The farmer's wives would always tell him to throw it away and give him a decent one. One day, however, he encountered the farmer at home. The farmer was just as horrified as his wife would have been: "Man, you can't eat that," he said. "Throw it away. Come round to the cow-shed wi' me and I'll find you a nice, fresh, hot one."

There is often more than a hint of salt-over-the-shoulder superstition involved. The Scots make jokes of the things they fear, like old age or death, as in the tale of Old MacPherson. To celebrate his 95th birthday, his cronies sent round an attractive young 'masseuse'. When he opened the door, she said brightly, "I'm here to give you super sex." He ruminated on this for a while, then finally said, "I'll ha'e the soup."

Though the Scots like a joke to have a point, the point should ideally not be too obvious. They relish above all the moment between the end of the joke and the laugh, (or at any rate the grimace), of the person to whom it is told, when the humour finally sinks in.

Their own idiosyncrasies can be targets for mockery. It was a Scottish playwright who made one of his characters say: "Son, I've been round the world, and Scotland is the only country where six and half a dozen are never the same thing." But no single place in Scotland is a butt for the humour of everyone else. The closest to an exception is Aberdeen, which has somehow acquired a reputation for excessive Scottish thriftiness: for example, "If a Scotsman opens his purse, the moths fly out. If an Aberdonian opens his purse, the moths are all dead."

Whilst the wits of Glasgow may sometimes mock the slow-thinking countryman, Scottish jokes are mainly at the expense of non-Scottish strangers, especially strangers who are too pleased with themselves. When an Australian came into an Edinburgh bar, he stood happily chatting for a time, then one of the regulars asked him, "Where are you from, pal?" "I'm from the finest country in the whole wide world," said the Aussie. "Is that so?" said the local. "You have a damn funny accent for a Scotsman."

From the hard edge of Scotland's urban culture comes a distinctive form of humour, personified in the life of 'Rab C. Nesbitt', an archetypal Glaswegian layabout with a paunch protruding from his string vest, unemployed, boozy, work-shy, male chauvinist to the nth degree, but always ready with a wisecrack. Other Scottish comedians, like Robbie Coltrane and Billy Connolly, have tapped this fruitful vein, as in Connolly's tale of the man who killed his wife and buried her in the back yard. He showed his friend, who said, "What did you leave her bum sticking out for?" And the man said, "I need somewhere to park my bike."

Culture

It sometimes strikes the observer that the Scots have done a great job in having things both ways. They're British when it suits them but also thoroughly Scots. This is true of their culture which comes in two quite separate forms. One is the shared cultural background of western Europe and with it all the world-wide resources of the English language. The other is the indigenous culture of Scotland itself. The Scots' contribution to the wider culture is modest compared to the part they have played in the development of science, industry and modern ways of thinking, but not negligible – least of all to the Scots themselves.

Scottish Music

Once the favourite instrument was the Celtic harp; now the fiddle, the piano accordion and the bagpipe form the basis of Scottish music, together with modern synthesisers and sound machines deplored by the purists. Aly Bain, the Shetland fiddler, has an international following, and he is one of a long line of expert Scottish fiddlers – up to a thousand fiddlers can gather together for special performances.

But the listeners far outnumber the players, and on Radio Scotland, Scottish Country Dance music featuring world-famous bands such as Jimmy Shand and His Band, gains large audiences. The Scots like to see and hear their national cultural heritage, rather than participate actively in it. And of course they consider themselves excellent judges. When a piper got up to play at a concert in Skye, a member of the audience shouted: "Sit down, ye useless cratur." The chairman rose to protest: "Who called the piper a useless cratur?" Back came the reply: "Who called the useless cratur a piper?"

The Scots have invented a form of music all their own, the 'great music' of the pibroch, played solo on the bagpipes. Composed according to strict rules of form and structure, it is the supreme test of a piper, and annual championships are held. Open to players from all nations, this is a global trophy which stays firmly in Scotland.

Scottish traditional music has been given a fillip by the recent interest in 'world' music, seeking for clear ethnic roots. Musicologists have detected a primitive element in the pentatonic scale of typical Scottish tunes that links them to a pre-Celtic, prehistoric musical tradition found also in Siberia and Mongolia. "When we sing 'Auld Lang Syne'," wrote one, "we may be perpetuating the melodic conventions of the Circumpolar Stone Age." Such a thought would give great satisfaction to the Scots.

Literature

Life in old-time Scotland being distinctly short on home comforts, it is no surprise that the country's first fiction writers turned away from bleak reality to the more agreeable land of fantasy. The novels of Walter Scott reinvented a harsh and bloody history as something colourful, dramatic and heroic.

These days it's New Realism. The lives of the unemployed, the drop-outs and the disaffected elements of city life in Glasgow and Edinburgh – lapped in a culture of drugs, drink and minor crime – have, ironically, made some writers of the 'bad boy' school famous and even wealthy. The irony is not lost on the writers themselves, like Irvine Welsh, whose *Trainspotting* brought Edinburgh into the international eye as something more than the gracious city of festival and flowers. Many Scots were surprised that such remorselessly Scots dialogue as:

"Wuv goat that cairry-oot tae organise, mind."
"Aye, right, What ye gittin?"
"Boatil ay voddy n a few cans."

could be an international hit. But the vigour of the new Scots fiction comes from tapping the underlying forceful strain that forms one strand of the national character and comes out sometimes in violence and aggressive behaviour. This writing feels real and true to life. Its subject matter also appears exotic – a culture not quite like any other. To an international public hungry for novelty, it is an exciting new taste.

Exiles and Stay-at-Homes

Some Scottish writers, like the Orcadian, George Mackay Brown, or the great Gaelic poet Sorley Maclean who taught in Wester Ross, achieved wide success while remaining very much part of their own locality. But it is striking that many Scottish creative artists of international fame have moved out of Scotland, like Muriel Spark, Edinburgh-born doyenne of novelists, who set up home in Tuscany, and fashion designers Jean Muir and Bill Gibb who lived in London. The exiles do not abandon the thought of Scotland. Robert Louis Stevenson went as far away as he possibly could, to Samoa in the South Pacific, where he spent a large part of his time lying on his verandah among the palm trees, dreaming of, and re-creating, the Scotland of his youth.

Scotland produces two kinds of creative artists – those who are nourished by living there, and those who are stifled. Even those who remain are often rebels and liable to be deemed eccentrics like the 'concrete poet' and landscape-artist Ian Hamilton Finlay, whose sculpture-poetry park is more honoured in Europe and America than in his home country, where he fought a long battle with the authorities to secure its existence. The prime example is, however, Hugh MacDiarmid, Scotland's greatest 20th-century poet, who got so far up the nose of the burghers of Langholm, his birthplace, that they refused to put up a memorial to him after his death.

Scottish artists often experience a lack of appreciation in their own country. It stems from a peculiar reluctance of the Scots to grant any special abilities to those who, in their opinion, have no right to be considered any better or more successful than anyone else. It is an attitude neatly summed up in the words "I kenned his faither".

Systems

Getting About

Every form of public transport is used in Scotland including the shortest scheduled air-flight in the world – the two-minute trip from one Orkney isle, Westray, to its neighbour, Papa Westray. On the Isle of Barra, where the landing strip is a beach, scheduled flights have to take account not only of the times of tides, but the clearing of the cows from the sand by the local crofter.

In outlying places, local transport, when it exists, is usually quite efficient, with post-buses carrying both passengers and the mail. Only a few of the Highlands' single track roads remain, thus removing a valuable source of conversation and complaint. On these narrow strips of asphalt, cars rocket towards each other (as if each had Jackie Stewart at the wheel) until one or other turns aside at the last moment into one of the occasional passing places. Sometimes slower drivers actually will pull into them and let you overtake – unless you hoot and flash at them, in which case they will hunch over the steering wheel and settle down in front of you to a steady 20 miles an hour. This is not the only hazard. Notices proclaim leaping deer, falling rocks and, more frequently, 'Unfenced Road: Beware of Sheep' – sheep having a tendency to settle down on the warm tarmac to doze.

Trains in Scotland are efficient and usually run to time. But there are not very many of them. Travel by public transport, particularly on a Sunday, requires time and patience, nowhere more so than on the long single-track rail and road routes through the glens and across the moors. On a train from Inverness to Glasgow, as it neared its destination and people began to assemble their belongings, a passenger remarked, "Well, that's the worst of the journey over." "Where are you going to?" asked his neighbour. "China," was the reply.

Education

The Scots respect cleverness and like to feel that they possess plenty of it themselves. In Scotland there is nothing wrong with being clever, so long as you show it by words or actions, rather than by bragging. You don't have to hide it. To say of someone that "he has a good conceit of himself" is neither praise nor blame, just a statement of fact.

Few countries have been more adept than Scotland at managing their own mythology and keeping it up to date. Its success is due to the fact that the Scots themselves believe it. This is certainly true of education, which in Scotland has always been separately run from the rest of the UK. It being Scotland, there are of course also sceptics who say that modern educational policy in Scotland is simply the policy that obtained in England ten years ago and is now outmoded there.

Behind the screen of myth, there is real concern about the quality and style of education. Schools are nowadays less disciplined than was the case a generation ago; teachers less respected than in the days when schoolboys were expected to salute, military-style, when passing them in the street. The true focus of this concern is the awareness that schools are factories producing the country's largest invisible export – brains.

Education is notionally democratic. But between the blazered and short-trousered primary schoolboys of the inner city fee-paying schools, and their jeans-and-anorak clad counterparts in state primary schools on outer city housing estates, there are great social and economic differences. The quality of teaching may be just as good in both schools, but the size of class and the resources available are very different. Outside the cities, virtually all children go to state schools, many of which are excellent in every respect. Secondary schools in Scotland are often called academies, but any other connections with Plato would be hard to find. Classics teachers are as common as hens' teeth, and Latin in the syllabus has been replaced by contemporary subjects like Sociology. Nearly all children are day-pupils. The boarding school tradition of England has never appealed to the Scots, and the few Scottish boarding schools tend to be inhabited by sons and daughters of well-to-do 'Anglo-Scots' and children sent from England for the benefits of Scottish fresh air and, of course, a Scottish education.

Some 44% of students in 1997 went on to college or university, where the Scottish honours course is a four-year one rather than the three years which applies in England and elsewhere. When university education ceased to be free, the London government was obliged to concede a free fourth year to students in Scotland.

Among Scotland's present 12 universities the ancient foundations inevitably have the most prestige. St Andrews and Edinburgh, especially, are very popular with English undergraduates, who provide almost half of each year's intake. This fact riles the Scots, even though it might be said to prove their belief that Scottish education is best.

Government

Devolution

Nearly 300 years after their Parliament voted to abolish itself in a union with England, the Scots voted in 1998 to have it back again, albeit with limited internal powers. For many Scots this was a first step towards an independent nation once more; for others, it was a step too far from the long-established Union, and the start of the break-up of the United Kingdom.

'Devolution' of internal government is a new experience for the Scots, who were previously free to moan about the shortcomings of the British parliament in London. In that body, with only 75 Scottish members out of more than 650, Scottish affairs were neglected, or mismanaged, by governments whose attention was fixed on England and the wider world. Now power to change things lies in the Scots' own hands. One thing is certain – the new Parliament will see some stormy debates. Even as Labour and Liberal-Democrat politicians formed a coalition in Scotland's first devolved 'executive', the Liberals were branding their new colleagues as liars.

In Scotland, which has always been more leftward-leaning than England, the political divide is not the conventional left versus right. Instead there are three centre-left parties: the Scot Nats (Scottish Nationalists), pushing for more and more independence, with the eventual aim of complete political separation from England; the Labour Party, as Unionists, trying to hold the line; the Liberal Democrats somewhere in between – and the Conservatives out on the fringe.

The electoral system for the Scottish Parliament was cunningly worked out to make it difficult for any party to have an absolute majority. Coalition politics will prevail, making a new order of things for politicians. They may even have to begin to listen to one another.

Administration

Democracy weighs heavily on the Scots. Five tiers of administration are piled above them: the district council, the regional council, the Scottish Parliament, the British Parliament, and the EU Commission and Parliament. At least three different voting systems are in use. The Scots need to keep their wits about them just to make sure they vote for the person they really want.

In rural areas, local politics are decorous, on the surface at least, but elsewhere things can get heated. The Lord Provost of Glasgow had to barricade himself in his opulently furnished office against furious members of his own party, and the burgh council of Paisley became a source of national entertainment when feuding Labour and Nationalist members traded insults, bringing the playground phrase 'ya bampot' (numbskull) into unaccustomed use.

Councils are viewed with suspicion. At the heart of this is the feeling that it may not be pure idealism and the desire to serve that motivates all local councillors. Scottish tribalism means that individuals or political parties can remain entrenched in powerful positions for a long time and begin to believe they are 'chiefs' by right rather than by permission. And chiefs have always dispensed favours to their faithful followers.

Curiously, despite all the layers of government, much of the country's affairs are run by unelected 'quangos' (quasi-autonomous-non-governmental agencies). These bodies, which range from the Scottish Arts Council to area health authorities and water boards, spend vast sums of public money. Although run by professionals, they are controlled by political appointees from among 'the great and the good'. The consequent atmosphere of self-congratulation and opportunities for quiet chicanery are observed with cynicism by the population at large: they have no access to expense accounts and celebratory lunches.

It remains to be seen whether the Parliament, still floundering in the effort to establish its role in national life, will change the established political culture, or become part of it. One thing is certain: the true seat of power will continue to be the headquarters of that secretive, silent and least accountable body of men and women – the Scottish Civil Service.

Royalty

Scotland is a kingdom, one of the oldest in Europe. Its crown and sceptre – known as the Honours of Scotland – are on display in Edinburgh Castle. It was a Scottish king, James VI, who went to London in 1603 to become the king in England as well.

Scots like to remind folk that their monarch is Queen, or King, of Scots – not of Scotland: a leader of the people, not the owner of the land. Mixed in with the nationalist and left-wing orientation of Scottish politics is a strong republican streak. The popularity of the royal family waxes and wanes, and they are seen as visitors rather than part of the fabric of the country. The royal Palace of Holyroodhouse is empty for much of the year. But for most Scots, especially when they look around at their elected representatives and speculate on how any of them would perform as President, the question of monarchy versus republic is not a live issue, even though an element is said to exist whose slogan is: 'Sean Connery for King'.

Law

The law is yet another area where Scots rejoice in their difference. In the Union of Scotland with England, the law and the Church were exempted from amalgamation with their English counterparts, and Scottish law remains distinct, closer to the Roman Law of continental Europe than to English Common Law.

Each area court has its Procurator Fiscal, or examining magistrate. The courts still have the unique verdict at their disposal, 'Not Proven' – which lets the accused person go free but with the clear inference that he or she is no better than he should be. In Scotland, you are assumed to be your own person, and to attempt suicide is not a crime. There are some quite specific Scottish offences, like 'hamesucken', which means breaking into a man's house in order to beat him up.

The country is divided into Sheriffdoms, with the Sheriff, a qualified lawyer, able to try all but the gravest cases. These go to the Court of Session which is based in Edinburgh but travels on circuit to the major towns. Eminent as they are, the judges of this highest court cannot emulate the flamboyant behaviour of such 18th-century predecessors as Lord Braxfield and his colleagues, who thought nothing of calling for bottles of port to sustain them through a long trial.

At lower levels, Scottish law produces some colourful figures, especially among the advocates (Scottish barristers), some of whom rely on personality and oratory, as much as the facts, to sway a jury. One of these, having by impassioned pleading secured a 'Not Guilty' verdict for a known felon, was complimented afterwards by his client: "You almost had me convinced of my own innocence."

Business

Once a land of heavy industry, its central valley packed with coal mines and steelworks, with the River Clyde the world's main shipbuilding centre, Scotland has seen all that vanish well within a single lifetime. Now more people are employed in service industries than in manufacturing; and women account for approximately half the work force.

Almost as their coal ran out, the Scots found they had some of the world's biggest offshore oil and gas deposits under the sea on their doorstep. The country rapidly became the world centre of advanced 'offshore' technology. The costly exploitation was done by the international oil giants, who also reaped the rewards.

The Scots claim a substantial corner in Information Technology, and the press was quick to call the central valley 'Silicon Glen' in emulation of the California original. The on-line era has transformed the Scottish Highlands from a remote and in some ways backward area into a buzzing district of the global village.

It was Scottish emigrants who turned Hong Kong into one of the world's great trading centres, yet the Scots are not among the world's great traders. They are better known for seeing their innovations developed successfully elsewhere. Kirkpatrick Macmillan, who built the world's first effective bicycle and rode on it from Dumfries to Glasgow (where he was prosecuted for causing a road accident) never pursued his invention. Henry Bell, the steamship pioneer, died in poverty. Another Bell, Patrick, built the first effective reaping machine, but it was eclipsed by the American McCormick's. John Logie Baird, pioneer of television, saw an alternative system to his become the standard.

There are few major enterprises still owned in Scotland by Scots. Most industry and business is partly or entirely owned elsewhere. The business cadre is managerial, acting on policy decided in Frankfurt, Seoul or Detroit. Banking and financial services are a major industry; if the Scots don't have vast amounts of wealth themselves, they certainly like looking after other people's.

Most Scottish businesses are small. Among the 2,000 largest companies, the average number of employees is 360, and of the nearly 300,000 companies registered in Scotland, the average staffing level is less than six. The traditional industries of Scotland, whisky and textiles, have survived the collapse of heavy industry, sustained by the unique nature and high quality of their products and by assiduous marketing. Tweed cloth from the Hebrides and the Borders is still a basic resource for the fashion industry, though thankfully modern processing techniques no longer require the steeping of raw fabric in stale urine, which used to contribute to the distinctive and pleasant aroma of Harris tweed.

Much energy is spent on the process of winning inward investment, that is, bribing foreign companies to set up in Scotland with huge capital grants and low rents. Empty factories and razed sites testify to the fleeting nature of such projects. But Scotland, by the size of its population and the need to provide jobs, is tied into the international game of wooing. The Scots play this game quite well, and draw on their assets whenever possible. It's not in every country that the visiting executives from head office can play on a world-class golf course, or catch a salmon from a tumbling river, only a short drive from the works.

Foresters and Fishermen

To the surprise of the visitor, a 'forest' in Scotland may be entirely tree-less, if it's a deer-forest. But great tracts of hillside are covered in woodland, and sanctuaries for birds and plants, such as the vast region of level bogland known as the 'Flow Country', are coveted by those who like to see empty landscapes populated by profitable trees. The growth of forestry as an important industry has had a mixed welcome. Serried ranks of Sitka spruce do not improve the view.

Another industry enduring its share of controversy is fishing. Hard-hit by over-fishing of the North Sea grounds and by European-imposed quotas, it employs far fewer men and boats than was once the case. Formerly important fishing harbours now hold little more than yachts and pleasure boats. Off the west coast, the horizon is lit up by the 'Klondikers' – huge fish factory ships, with their attendant trawlers – from as far away as Japan.

Closer inshore, fish farms have been established in

many sea-lochs. As the wild salmon becomes rarer and more expensive, the farmed variety becomes ever more plentiful. Shellfish too are grown like a crop. The Scots who went out on open-decked fishing boats in oilskins and sou' westers are more likely nowadays to wear white coats and be hand-feeding a hundred thousand baby lobsters, each in its separate little compartment.

Farmers and Crofters

The oldest business of Scotland is farming. The Aberdeen-Angus bull, the Ayrshire cow, the Cheviot sheep, the Clydesdale horse, all testify to Scotland's role in the development of modern agriculture. Most urban Scots are countryfolk at heart. Older people reminisce about the October 'tattie holidays' when schools closed for two weeks and the children helped to harvest potatoes, earning enough money to pay for their new winter clothes and boots.

Farmers are a close-knit community; many farms are single-family operations, with neighbours helping one another out with major tasks like harvesting and planting. It's not entirely an open-air life. All farmers have, it is said, become experts in accountancy, if only to keep abreast of European bureaucracy and ensure that they get the maximum possible amount of subsidy. The farmer sits indoors scratching his head at his computer and calculator, while his wife is out in the fields, driving the giant-wheeled tractor.

In the Highlands and Islands, the typical agricultural unit is the croft, a tiny one-man farm, or as some have it, 'a piece of ground entirely surrounded by regulations'. Often uneconomic in themselves, there is a whole system of grants and subsidies to support the crofts, but most crofters have another job as well, such as local teacher, or taxi-driver, or maker of finely tuned violins.

The lure of remote life has transformed some moribund West Highland communities into active places. It is quite normal nowadays to enter a croft house and find it occupied by an ecologist with his own internet web site, giving advice to someone in Saskatchewan.

Language

Scots and English

The Scots like to remember the fact that they once spoke a distinct kind of English, called Scots, and to many outsiders it seems they still do. Sir James Murray, the Scots founder of the *Oxford English Dictionary*, compiled a Scots Grammar, because even at the end of the 19th century he saw so many different usages in his native country. These were not wrong, he realised, but, like so much else, different.

Today, the Scots speak standard English, more or less. What is left of the Scots language is now an endangered species, to the point that schools, which once tried to beat it out of the children, now have it as a special subject.

Even modern poems written in Scots are published with glossaries to explain such phrases as: 'Bumpity doun in the corrie gaed whuddran the pitiless whunstane'. (The pitiless whinstone went rushing bumpily down into the mountain hollow.)

Scots speech is garnished with words that are exclusively and distinctively Scots. Most are expressive. Even a non-Scot has no trouble in understanding what is meant by *dreich* weather, or its opposite, a *braw* day. A *snell* wind is one that penetrates, and a *gurly* sea is not for pleasure trips. To be *couthy* is to be the salt of the earth, a bit rough and ready perhaps, but that's almost a virtue. To keep a *trig* house means it's properly neat and tidy, but a lady who hears herself defined as *perjink* has been found to be just a bit too fastidious in her manner. This is better than being *clarty*, or dirty, or being the kind of slovenly woman dismissed as "just a *gether-up*". Anything that is a regular nuisance is a *perfect scunner*.

The old tongue reaches deep into the Scottish psyche, and Scots words leap to the lips in moments of stress or emotion. Lovers are *dearies*. Children are *weans* and *bairns*. Silly people are *numpties*, while a person of common sense has *mense* or *smeddum*. The pale and sickly look *peelie-wally*, the day-dreamer is in a *dwam*, someone with too much to do is *trachled*, and if everything is too much, he might go *clean gyte*.

While many Scots words are common to the whole nation, others are used only in certain districts and instantly show where the speaker comes from. Thus in the north-east, laddies and lassies become *loons* and *quines*. In all parts there is regular practice of the Scottish diminutive. '*Wee*' is a much loved word, and the -ie ending is often thrown in for good measure. A *wee loonie* in Aberdeen is not a vertically challenged madman but a little boy.

Scottish accents communicate a range of values. Telephone sales companies like to employ speakers with what they call an 'educated Scots' accent. Its clarity and precision give their message a sense of reliability and sincerity. At the other end of the scale, that of Glasgow has few friends. It remains the most impenetrable to strangers, though if more visited Shetland, or rural Aberdeenshire where they would encounter the local 'Doric', they might be even more baffled. The Scots themselves find a guide to Glasgow-speak very useful, and *Parliamo Glasgow*, with its explanations of such phrases as, JIWANNABELTOANRAMOOTH?, translated as 'Do you want a punch in the mouth?', is never out of print.

The Gaeltachd

New arrivals in the Highland administrative region are slightly daunted by large notices in Gaelic, welcoming them to the *Gaeltachd* ('country of the Gaels'). This arouses expectation of kilted figures, not merely leaping out from behind boulders, but shouting incomprehensible remarks, perhaps even threats or insults. Here they find a language gap beside which the English-Scots one is the merest crack. They need have no fears. Unless they venture to the Outer Hebrides, their chance of hearing Gaelic spoken as an everyday language is about as great as hearing Mandarin Chinese. Gaelic today is spoken by about 80,000 (1.6% of the population). The last monoglot Gaelic speakers died early in the 20th century.

Six hundred years ago Gaelic was the language of the whole country, except for Anglo-Saxon Lothian. It has been fighting a long rearguard action. But just before it is too late, there is some recognition that a huge part of Scottish history and culture is wrapped up in the Gaelic language, and to lose that would be like losing half the country's identity. Hundreds of years of Scotland's past are preserved in Gaelic, a living language which over 98% of Scots do not understand. It is like being in a house with a locked-up room that is never referred to and to which some elderly and undesirable relative has been banished.

Nor does it relate only to the culture of bygone and very different times. Some of Scotland's finest modern poetry is in Gaelic. Whilst it is never likely to be an everyday language again, there is a resurgence of Gaelic teaching and writing. In the Highlands, a generation ago, the parents used to talk Gaelic for not-in-front-of-the-children topics. Now in many cases, the children, profiting from Gaelic classes at school, do the same for subjects unfitted to adult ears.

The Author

David Sutherland Ross is a fully fledged member of that well-established species, the Scottish literary exile. Born in Oban, Argyll, he was removed at an early age to his ancestral county of Ross and Cromarty, where he grew up and went to school. Furnished with a little knowledge about all sorts of things thanks to a Scottish education, he migrated to London expecting to become a journalist, but became a publisher instead.

Having learned from blurb-writing how to represent a tangle of ill-assorted elements and random events as a unified whole, he realised he was eminently qualified to write the history of Scotland, and produced *Scotland: History of a Nation*. Nowadays, as chairman of a small Scottish-based publishing company, he combines publishing with writing and the compilation of anthologies, including *Awa' and Bile Yer Heid*, a collection of Scottish insults and invective. Although he enjoys it all immensely, sometimes he wonders whether it isn't too late to try something completely different, like utilising his ability to do water-divining; or perhaps opening a beach restaurant in Bali.

His favourite place in Scotland is the summit of Ben Venue; his favourite Scottish food, new-baked scones with raspberry jam; his favourite Scottish book, *The Scottish National Dictionary*, and his favourite Scottish phrase, "Just a sensation."